DATE DUE			

42229

333.73
REG

Regan, Michael.

Bringing back our tundra

WARREN CENTRAL HIGH SCHOOL
VICKSBURG MISSISSIPPI 39180

BRINGING BACK OUR
TUNDRA

BY MICHAEL REGAN

CONTENT CONSULTANT

Dr. Jeffrey M Welker
UArctic Research Chair
Professor of Arctic Ecology
University of Oulu, Finland & University
of Alaska Anchorage

Essential Library
An Imprint of Abdo Publishing
abdopublishing.com

CONSERVATION
SUCCESS STORIES

abdopublishing.com

Published by Abdo Publishing, a division of ABDO, PO Box 398166, Minneapolis, Minnesota 55439. Copyright © 2018 by Abdo Consulting Group, Inc. International copyrights reserved in all countries. No part of this book may be reproduced in any form without written permission from the publisher. Essential Library™ is a trademark and logo of Abdo Publishing.

Printed in the United States of America, North Mankato, Minnesota
102017
012018

THIS BOOK CONTAINS
RECYCLED MATERIALS

Cover Photo: Tony Campbell/Shutterstock Images
Interior Photos: Arthur Max/AP Images, 4, 6, 8–9, 99; Shutterstock Images, 10, 41 (background), 54–55, 62, 76, 88; Bryan and Cherry Alexander/Science Source, 12–13, 18; FLPA/Alamy, 14; Red Line Editorial, 17; Ron Niebrugge/Alamy, 21; Stephen J. Krasemann/Science Source, 23; Phil Degginger/Science Source, 24–25; Itar-Tass/ZumaPress/Newscom, 26, 98 (middle right); Diana Haecker/AP Images, 28–29, 98 (bottom right); Goddard Photography/iStockphoto, 31; Vadim Nefedoff/Shutterstock Images, 32; Jeff McGraw/iStockphoto, 34; W. Kruck/iStockphoto, 37; Jonathan Raa/Newzulu/Alamy, 38; iStockphoto, 41 (top left), 41 (top right), 41 (bottom left), 49, 51 (top), 53, 58, 64, 84, 97; Martin Hejzlar/Shutterstock Images, 41 (bottom right); NPS Photo, 42, 68, 98 (top right); Louie Lea/iStockphoto, 46–47; Tony Campbell/Shutterstock Images, 51 (bottom); Charles Helm, 56; Trent Ernst, Eye For Detail Photography, 59; blickwinkel/Alamy, 60–61; Vladimir Melnikov/Shutterstock Images, 66–67, 98 (left); Wendy Olsen Photography/iStockphoto, 70–71; Vladimir Melnik/Shutterstock Images, 73; Fred Hirschmann/SuperStock, 74; Hudson Bay Project/KRT/Newscom, 78–79; Andrea and Antonella Ferrari/NHPA/Photoshot/Newscom, 80–81; Uwe Bergwitz/iStockphoto, 82; Arndt Sven-Erik/Arterra Picture Library/Alamy, 86; YARA/Kongsberg/Cover Images/Newscom, 90; Ashley Cooper/Alamy, 92–93; Nice Kim/Shutterstock Images, 94–95

Editor: Marie Pearson
Series Designer: Laura Polzin

Publisher's Cataloging-in-Publication Data

Names: Regan, Michael, author.
Title: Bringing back our tundra / by Michael Regan.
Description: Minneapolis, Minnesota : Abdo Publishing, 2018. | Series: Conservation success stories |Includes online resources and index.
Identifiers: LCCN 2017946792 | ISBN 9781532113178 (lib.bdg.) | ISBN 9781532152054 (ebook)
Subjects: LCSH: Tundra ecology--Juvenile literature. | Restoration ecology--Juvenile literature. | Conservation of natural resources--Juvenile literature.
Classification: DDC 333.78216--dc23
LC record available at https://lccn.loc.gov/2017946792

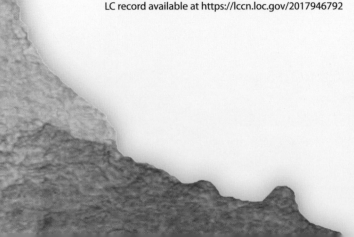

CONTENTS

Nikita Zimov is a scientist who studies the tundra in Siberia.

TUNDRA: THE COLDEST ENVIRONMENT

In April 2011, Nikita Zimov was in a hurry. He jumped into his truck loaded with six live elk. He had to get from Novosibirsk, a major city in southern Siberia, to the Arctic town of Chersky to meet his father, Sergey. The trip was 2,500 miles (4,000 km), and time was not on his side. The frozen rivers that served as winter roads in northern Siberia were about to thaw as summer approached. He sped along the winding river road. He passed many white wooden crosses that marked

Sergey Zimov shows how methane can be stored under frozen lakes.

the spots where drivers had died. After two weeks, and only 25 miles (40 km) from his destination, the truck's brakes gave out, and Zimov hit a snowbank. The truck tipped over. Luckily, neither Zimov nor the six elk were injured. He called his father on his cell phone, and after a cold and exhausting four-hour wait, help arrived.

REWILDING THE TUNDRA

Why did Zimov risk such a perilous journey to deliver six elk? The animals were key to a tundra experiment. He, his father, and other scientists from across the world have been conducting this study. The Zimovs and their associates had found that Earth's northern permafrost, the permanently frozen ground of the tundra, contained more than 1.1 trillion short tons (1 trillion metric tons) of carbon dioxide and methane.[1] Those gases are two of the carbon-based ingredients that keep Earth warm enough for humanity to survive. However, current climate change results in warmer temperatures that thaw tundra permafrost. As the permafrost thaws, large amounts of carbon dioxide and methane may be released into the atmosphere, speeding up climate change.

For more than 20 years, Sergey Zimov has worked on an experiment that would return the currently frozen moss- and lichen-covered ground to the grasslands that existed when mammoths and saber-toothed cats roamed more than 13,000 years ago. Zimov believes that restoring the

Permafrost extends downward nearly 1,476 feet (450 m).[3]

tundra to grasslands would insulate the permafrost and keep it from thawing. The frozen ground would keep the carbon from escaping into the atmosphere. Zimov and other scientists are testing whether grazing animals, such as elk, reindeer, horses, bison, and musk ox, could bring back the grasslands. This is called rewilding. The experiment is conducted at the Northeast Science Station (NESS), a 34,600-acre (14,000 ha) reserve in northern Siberia.[4]

REWILDING

The original idea of rewilding came in 1998 with the article "Rewilding and Biodiversity" by Michael E. Soulé and Reed Noss. They referred to it as restoring big wilderness areas by reintroducing especially large predators. Russian rewilding expert Sergey Zimov refers to it as restoring large plant eaters to the tundra to reduce permafrost thawing. These plant and meat eaters require very large land areas to be effective. In the long term, both types of animals would be needed to provide the balance of nature necessary to ensure the survival of the tundra grasslands.

The Yakutian horse is a large grazing animal that lives at the NESS.

In 2015, Zimov's experiment seemed to be working, at least on a small scale. On a 124-acre (50 ha) area within the reserve, grasses had replaced the original tundra plants. Seventy plant eaters were helping prevent the permafrost from thawing. Grasses are better at reflecting continuous summer sunshine than trees or lichens. This helps keep the ground colder. During the winter snowy season, the animals keep the ground exposed to the frigid Arctic air. They do this by tramping down the snow, making it a poor insulator. They also sweep away the snow to eat the grasses beneath. Temperature measurements showed the grazed area's permafrost was 3.6 degrees Fahrenheit (2°C) colder than nongrazed areas.[5] According to Nikita Zimov, that would be enough to keep the permafrost solid.

ALPINE TUNDRA

Alpine tundra is found around the world in high mountain altitudes. The high reaches of the Andes mountains in Peru, the Himalayas in Nepal, and the Rocky Mountains of Canada and the United States are examples where alpine tundra exists. Trees cannot grow there. Like the Arctic tundra, short, small plants survive. Some of the animals that live on the alpine tundra include mountain goats, elk, and marmots, pictured.

REAL SOLUTION OR DAYDREAM?

Sergey Zimov's experiment is groundbreaking in tundra conservation. But for his experiment to preserve the tundra permafrost, the experiment would need to be greatly expanded. Millions of large plant-eating animals would need to be reintroduced to the tundra in Siberia. It would take decades to accomplish this. Many nations would need to work together to prevent the disastrous permafrost carbon release. But in 2015, Terry Chapin, an ecologist at the University of Alaska Fairbanks, pointed out that only two solutions to preserving the permafrost had been put forward. One was to cut global greenhouse gas emissions. The other was to implement Zimov's research.

TUNDRA RESEARCH STATION

The NESS was founded in 1989. Sergey Zimov and his son Nikita Zimov run the station. In addition to the scientists, Nikita Zimov's wife, three children, and other family members live at the station. The location of the NESS gives great access to the Russian tundra for scientific study. Funding for the station comes from the Russian Science Foundation, the US Department of Energy, the National Science Foundation, and the Soros Foundation.

WHAT IS THE TUNDRA?

Tundra is a treeless landscape found above the Arctic circle and in the alpine regions of high mountains globally. It is covered with short grasses, sedges (or marsh plants), forbs (flowering herbs that are not grasses), and small shrubs. In the Northern Hemisphere, Arctic tundra stretches across parts of northern Canada, Alaska, Siberia, Greenland, and Scandinavia. In the Southern Hemisphere, it covers Antarctic islands, the high mountains in Chile, and southern Chile and Argentina. Scientists often categorize tundra into Arctic tundra, which is in the northern hemisphere; Antarctic tundra in the southern hemisphere; and alpine tundra, which is in the mountains.

The tundra landscape may be one of Earth's youngest biomes. A biome is an area on Earth that has plants and animals that have adapted to living in the climate of that area. The tundra is believed to be approximately 10,000 years old, forming during and after the last

ice age. The tundra biome makes up 20 percent of Earth's surface.[6]

Winter in the tundra lasts up to ten and a half months, often beginning in late September and lasting until early June in the Northern Hemisphere.[7] It is bitterly cold, and portions of the soil are permanently frozen. In Arctic tundra, the sun may stay completely below the southern horizon for days. Winter temperatures average from -20 degrees Fahrenheit (-29°C) to -30 degrees Fahrenheit (-34°C). During the short summer season near Earth's poles, the sun shines 24 hours a day. Summer only lasts six to ten weeks. Even during the summer, tundra temperatures do not go above 54 degrees Fahrenheit (12.2°C).[8] The summer warmth thaws the top layer of soil. This is called the active layer. During the summer, the tundra supports many ecosystems. Wet sedge ecosystems lie along lakes and rivers and support sedges; moist areas not near lakes or rivers support small shrubs, mosses, and lichen; and dry upland

Many plants lie dormant during the long tundra winters.

INSECTS

One summer visitor to the tundra either thrills or bugs all the other animals—mosquitoes. During the continuous summer sunlight, the top layer of soil thaws. But because the land is flat and frozen underneath, deeper ground can't absorb the water. This is a perfect breeding ground for mosquitoes. As the summer season expands, the number of mosquitoes explodes. Many birds eat them, but the insects bite the mammals and humans who live or work on the tundra.

ecosystems are rocky with well-drained soil and also support small shrubs and lichens but not mosses. Many kinds of animals visit the tundra only during the summer, including migratory geese, caribou, and songbirds.

MANY COUNTRIES CONCERNED

Private organizations, university scientists, and government agencies in Canada, the United States, Russia, and Scandinavia are concerned about the effects of climate change on the Arctic and alpine tundra. The Wildlife Conservation Society Canada researches possible solutions for the problem. It works with the Arctic Council on projects to determine the effects of climate change on plants and animals in the tundra. The Arctic Council is an international political organization of Arctic nations. It also encourages broader conservation efforts to preserve the tundra biome.

The conservation efforts by government and private organizations to preserve the tundra and other ecosystems around the world have run into opposition. Some oil drilling and mining corporations and small government champions, who oppose government regulations of any kind, have put forth strong resistance to government conservation guidelines. This is particularly true in the United States. The resistance is partially because some people disagree that human activities are causing the changes. They also don't agree about what, if anything, needs to be done.

Yet the Arctic is warming faster than other areas on Earth. The North Slope of Alaska, for example, has warmed more than 5.4 degrees Fahrenheit (3°C) over the past 60 years.[9] In comparison, the Earth as a whole has increased 1.3 degrees Fahrenheit (0.7°C) over the last century.[10] Regardless of the cause, a thawing tundra has the potential to release vast amounts of greenhouse gases, contributing to more climate change. The result could be catastrophic for life on Earth. Conservation efforts on the tundra to keep the permafrost from thawing are vital to a livable climate on earth.

GREENHOUSE GASES MATCH RISING GLOBAL TEMPERATURES

In 2006, a documentary film titled *An Inconvenient Truth* raised the public's awareness of the dangers of climate change. The film stated climate change was caused by people and could lead to the collapse of industrial civilization. In 2007, the Intergovernmental Panel on Climate Change (IPCC) released a report saying the rise in world temperatures is directly related to the increase in greenhouse gas concentrations. In 2014, the IPCC went further and stated that continued greenhouse gas emissions will likely result in severe and widespread impacts on people that cannot be reversed. The IPCC is made up of thousands of independent scientists from around the world. Both the IPCC and former US vice president Al Gore, the writer and star of the film *An Inconvenient Truth*, were awarded the Nobel Peace Prize in 2007 for their work in climate science.

CARBON SINK

The tundra was one place on Earth that was known as a carbon dioxide sink. A carbon dioxide sink is a natural system that absorbs more carbon dioxide, a greenhouse gas, from the atmosphere than it releases. The biggest carbon sinks are plants, the oceans, and soil. Plants use the carbon dioxide for photosynthesis to grow. Some of that carbon is transferred to the soil when roots grow and die or when leaves fall to the ground. The tundra stores lots of carbon dioxide and methane in frozen ground.

For thousands of years, natural carbon dioxide sinks balanced the amount of carbon dioxide in the atmosphere. But when industries started burning mass amounts of coal during the Industrial Revolution in the 1800s, the balance was broken. The temperature of the atmosphere began to increase due to the excess carbon. By the 1900s, drilling for oil, clearing forests for farming, and burning fossil fuels for transportation only added to the problem. Today, warmer temperatures thaw permafrost, releasing carbon dioxide. The tundra now releases more carbon than it absorbs. To help slow climate change, some scientists would like to increase plant, ocean, and soil carbon sequestration, a process that removes carbon from the atmosphere.

Scientists are also investigating how to artificially capture and store carbon dioxide. With artificial carbon sequestration, carbon emissions are captured where they occur. That carbon is sometimes injected deep into the ocean. The idea is that the pressure and temperature of the ocean will keep the carbon dioxide there where it can dissolve into the seawater. Artificial sequestration is expensive, uses a lot of energy, and is untested to a large degree. Some argue it would be simpler to stop burning fossil fuels.

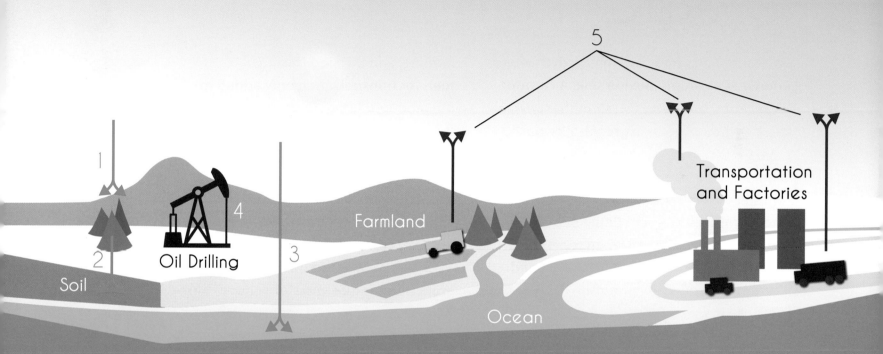

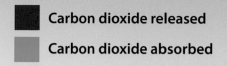
1. Plants absorb carbon dioxide.
2. The carbon dioxide is transferred to the soil where it is stored.
3. The ocean absorbs carbon dioxide.
4. Drilling for oil brings up carbon stored throughout Earth's history.
5. Burning fossil fuels to clear land for farms and to run vehicles and factories releases large amounts of carbon into the atmosphere.

Human activities such as drilling for oil or gas can rip up fragile tundra.

WHAT'S HAPPENING?

The tundra is at risk from both internal and external factors. Animals, plants, the land, and the seashores are all facing enormous challenges. Man-made structures, overkill of animals, surface disturbances, and pollution are breaking down the tundra. Climate change, invasive species, and threats to migratory birds' and animals' wintering and travel routes all harm the health of the Arctic.

ARCTIC REPORT CARD 2016

In 2016, the US National Oceanic and Atmospheric Administration (NOAA) released a report on the arctic tundra. The report said arctic tundra air temperatures were

GREEN ARCTIC

The Arctic is experiencing later winters and earlier springs. Pieter Beck, a vegetative ecologist, along with other scientists, studied what happens when higher temperatures lessen snow on tundra. The results revealed that the land will warm up, shrubs and larger trees will grow larger in size and territory, and the whole biome will become greener. Non-native plants would move in. Those changes can affect the entire globe. As the Arctic heats up, weather patterns will change. Extreme weather, such as large hurricanes and huge snowstorms, could become more common in highly populated areas. Dr. Jeffrey Welker from the University of Alaska Anchorage and his team have linked Arctic change to changes in winter snowstorms in the northeastern United States. As the Arctic warms, air currents become unstable. Cold Arctic air dips into the northeastern United States and delivers snowfall that would have ordinarily fallen in the Arctic.

"The Arctic region, the barometer of global climate change, is like an environmental early warning system of the world."[4]

—Klaus Töpfer, executive director of the United Nations Environment Programme, 2004

increasing at double the rate of the rest of the globe. The average temperature was the highest since records began in 1900. Since the beginning of the 1900s, the average temperature in arctic areas has increased 6.3 degrees Fahrenheit (3.5°C).[1]

Satellite pictures from 2016 show the tundra is getting greener during the summers. The plant-growing season used to last 50 to 60 days.[2] In Greenland, it is now 30 to 40 days longer—almost twice as long.[3] While this means those plants take up more carbon dioxide during the summer, the ground releases even more greenhouse gases. The overall effect is more greenhouse gases, which speeds up climate change.

FRAGILE PERMAFROST

Permafrost on the tundra seems to be very strong and stable. Even during the short summer, only the thin, active layer thaws. However, climate change, off-road vehicles, road building, mining operations, and oil and gas drilling reduce its stability. These activities lead to the heating and thawing of underlying ice in the permafrost. This thawing can result in the collapse of the surface and can also expose deeper levels of ice to thawing. The deeper ice has very large quantities of greenhouse gases that can be released into the atmosphere.

REINDEER HERDERS SEE CHANGES

Warmer weather is reshaping the tundra landscape. The tundra is normally cold and treeless. Climate change could cause trees from zones that are more temperate to grow farther into the tundra and shrubs to grow larger. The first signs of this were reported by reindeer herders in the Eurasian Arctic. The herders said they were losing sight of their reindeer because shrubs in their area were growing taller.

Nearly 30 years ago, tundra shrubs never grew more than 3.3 feet (1 m) tall. Now, in the area between Finland and western Siberia, shrubs are growing to twice that size.[5] That's big enough to hide a reindeer.

THAWING PERMAFROST IN ALASKA

In Alaska, 80 percent of the land has permafrost underneath it. Uneven sinking of the ground because of permafrost thaw, called subsidence, is a problem for 70 percent of Alaska. Over the next 20 years, scientists estimate this uneven sinking will cost Alaska an additional $3.6 to $6.1 billion to maintain roads, buildings, pipelines, airports, and water and sewage systems.[6]

COOLING ROADS

Roadways can cause permafrost to thaw. Simply clearing vegetation and building road embankments allows the permafrost below to warm. This results in sinking and damage to the roads once they are completed. It also releases more greenhouse gases into the atmosphere. Cooperation on a short highway project in Alaska demonstrated that these problems could be avoided.

Road engineers and University of Alaska scientists worked together to develop techniques to ensure the permafrost below the roads stayed frozen. One solution was using vents that allowed warm air to escape into the cold arctic air, thus pulling cold air into the roadbed, keeping the ground frozen. Another technique was to build devices that pulled heat from the permafrost during the winter months and then released it into the arctic air. Yet another strategy was building the road during the coldest winter months. Lower levels of the road were built in layers, allowing each layer to freeze solid before the next was added. This technique avoided the problem of introducing heat into the permafrost that happens when roads are built during the summer months.

Some tundra roads in Yukon, Canada, use ventilation pipes to keep the permafrost cool.

Satellite images and on-site scientific expeditions supported the herders' observations. In time, scientists believe continued warming in the area will allow forests to creep farther north into the tundra. This forest expansion could eventually lead to more warming soils and permafrost thawing.

In 2013, reindeer herders in northern Russia almost fell into a giant hole. Within a year, two more holes were discovered. One was 13 feet (4 m) wide and as deep as 330 feet (100 m).[7] At first, no one knew how the holes formed. However, villagers in the area reported seeing smoke in the area and then a flash of light in the sky before the first hole was discovered. There were several theories about how the holes were formed. These ranged from asteroid strikes to underground missile explosions to climate change. Russian scientist Anna Kurchatova explained that the thawing permafrost in the tundra allowed underground gas pockets to explode upward.

Tundra freezes and thaws unevenly, creating unique landscapes.

Unusual craters are located in the Yamal Peninsula in Russia.

This would have released stored carbon dioxide and methane gas.

ALASKAN VILLAGE IS MELTING

The temperatures on Sarichef Island off the northern coast of Alaska are warming. The Inupiat tribe of Inuit live in the village Shishmaref on the island. For decades, the villagers have watched how warming temperatures changed the conditions of the sea ice on the coast and permafrost in the land. Whole houses have fallen into the sea. Others have had to be moved to safer ground.

The disappearing sea ice has made hunting and fishing so difficult that villagers cannot gather enough food for the winter. In August 2016, the villagers voted to leave their ancestral home and move to the mainland to save themselves. When they move, they will have to give up their way of life. According to a study by the US Government Accountability Office, 31 other Alaskan villages face a similar fate.[8]

OTHER TUNDRA THREATS

In 2015, Alaska had one of its worst wildfire seasons in history. More than 5 million acres (2 million ha) of tundra and forest burned before the fire season ended.

METHANE GAS

When people burn fossil fuel, it produces methane gas. Methane gas is a greenhouse gas just as carbon dioxide is. Both trap heat when released into the atmosphere. However, methane is more potent than carbon dioxide because it traps more heat. Over a 20-year period, methane gas traps 86 percent more heat than carbon dioxide.[9] Methane's quick impact on climate change may be irreversible in the long term.

The Greenland ice sheet has been measured for 37 years. In 2016, it had its second-earliest spring melt.[10]

Normally, fires in Alaska burn approximately 1 million acres (405,000 ha) each year.[11] Scientists fear that global climate change could cause even worse fires in the future because of drying tundra, thawing permafrost, and lower snowpack. Burning trees and other plants release huge amounts of carbon into the atmosphere, adding to already-increasing greenhouse gas emissions from other sources throughout the world.

In addition to thawing permafrost, other forces and activities have been shown to have harmful effects on tundra. Ozone depletion at the North and South Poles allows stronger ultraviolet rays to

RIVER PIRACY

In Canada's Yukon, unusually warm spring weather in 2016 caused a big change. Rapidly melting water carved a canyon through a glacier's ice. The canyon diverted the water from its usual river route to the Bering Sea in the north. It instead flowed to the Alsek River, dumping the water into the Pacific Ocean to the south. Scientists call this river piracy. The reroute took just a few months. Scientists were startled by its suddenness. Usually, such a change takes thousands of years. Climate change was blamed for this.

Shore erosion has destroyed homes in Shishmaref.

29

ANTARCTICA IN TROUBLE

Few people live permanently in Antarctica, so nearly all its problems come from the environment. The West Antarctica peninsula is one of the fastest-warming places on earth. Penguin populations in Antarctica are declining because their main source of food, krill, is disappearing. Scientists report that climate change is causing Antarctic ice cover loss. Vast amounts of ice are melting in some regions. In 2017, a piece of ice the size of the state of Delaware broke off from an ice shelf in Antarctica. Scientists cannot directly tie the break with warmer temperatures, but they fear it forecasts the coming disappearance of the shelf. The ice loss reduces ice algae, which is the main food source for krill.

penetrate the atmosphere, resulting in damage to the tundra. Air pollution from blowing dust and human activities contaminates the plants on the tundra. Many animals eat the contaminated plants. Mining, extracting oil and gas, and building and using roads can interfere with wildlife travel routes and cause damage to the upper layers of the tundra.

A 2017 study of water on Antarctica shows there is more melting happening there than previously thought. The study, by Columbia University's Lamont-Doherty Earth Observatory, used satellite images from the early 1970s and aerial photography from the late 1940s to the present. The researchers believe melt water will speed up ice loss in Antarctica. This affects both sea and land animals around and on that continent. In addition, Antarctica is becoming greener. Researchers discovered rapidly growing areas of mosses on the northern peninsula of the icy continent. Soil samples found dramatic changes of more than four to five times more growth over the last 150 years.[12] The changes were blamed on human-caused climate change.

The forces currently at work on the tundra ecosystem can lead to great climate and geographical changes throughout the rest of the globe. Local and regional conservation

Moss growth on Antarctica's northern peninsula has been increasing since the 1960s.

projects, along with international cooperative efforts, may still lessen the effects of the damage already done. Those same efforts may help the world adapt to global changes that cannot be fixed.

"I think using the word 'crisis' is appropriate."[13]

—*Bill Erasmus, Canadian Arctic Athabaskan Council representative, describing the damage being done to the tundra, 2009*

Some Inuit live in Nuuk, Greenland.

Chapter
THREE

TUNDRA VALUES

In the 2010s, the Arctic was home to more than 4 million people. Climate change affects the Arctic more intensely than other areas of the globe. As a result, residents feel the effects more intensely and immediately than people living in other areas. The Arctic is home to the Inuit of North America, while northern Europe, Russia, and Scandinavia are home to the Sami. More than 50 different indigenous groups live in the Arctic. At least 40 of those live along the northern areas of Russia and on the Aleutian Islands.[1] In some places, preserves have been formed, so these people live life as they have throughout history.

VALUES REFLECTION

Since the early 1900s, parks and protected sites in the Arctic have also been set aside for their natural value, including habitat for wildlife. For thousands of years,

CARIBOU

Caribou, also known as reindeer, migrate around the tundra in their thick, furry coats. They have large hooves that help them travel on snow and marshy areas. The hooves help them dig through the snow to reach food. Their hooves also help them swim. Caribou can cross wide, freezing rivers. Their fur keeps the icy water from reaching their skin.

caribou, musk ox, polar bears, arctic foxes, snowy owls, lemmings, migrating birds, and other animals have lived and had offspring in the tundra. All the while, their habitat stayed the same. Preserving a habitat means preserving the wildlife. The tundra's unique geology and natural beauty are also important to preserve for current and future generations' enjoyment.

Several other things make the tundra a valuable place. The tundra's role in regulating world temperatures makes it important on a global scale. The tundra biome is important for scientific research. Research helps scientists understand the natural environment and what happens because of human-caused changes. Teaching and training people about their natural surroundings and the great diversity of plants and animals provides educational opportunities on the tundra.

However, some of the tundra's resources can put it at risk for human disturbance. Taking resources, such as oil, from the tundra may harm the environment unless carefully handled. Even sport hunting and recreational activities, such as hiking, camping, and photography, can either contribute to the public's understanding of the tundra or hinder its preservation through habitat damage.

CHALLENGES FACING ARCTIC PROTECTED AREAS

In 2010, there were more than 1,100 protected areas in the Arctic worldwide. They covered a total of 1.4 million square miles (3.5 million sq km). Some people think this should be enough to protect the entire biome. However, this is misleading. There is very little protection of the Arctic oceans. In addition, Greenland's National Park accounted for more than 40 percent of protected land.[2]

TUNDRA PLANTS

Because of the frozen ground on the tundra, plant roots have very little space to grow. Despite that, more than 1,700 species of plants live on the tundra.[3] Although some flowering plants, herbs, and grasses can survive the tundra weather, the plants that can best survive are small shrubs, algae, lichens, fungi, and moss. The most common vegetation is small plants that grow close to the ground and close together. This helps them resist cold weather and avoid windblown snow and ice. Being close to the ground also gives them more heat to grow during the summer. The plants provide food for the animals that live on and migrate to the tundra.

One challenge to increasing protected areas is funding. This includes funds for staff and governing organizations. There must also be strong rule enforcement along with political and local support for these areas. This is not happening in many areas of the Arctic.

Attitudes about Arctic protected areas have recently changed, presenting a challenge to its conservation. In the past, the protected areas were very remote. They seemed to be of little value to anyone but those who might live there. More recently, though, the Arctic has gained the attention of oil, gas, mining, forestry, and transportation businesses. As a result, there is growing pressure to allow resource extraction companies to take from protected areas, since these companies bring jobs and income. Today, people face the challenge of balancing sustainable jobs and income while preserving the environment.

CONFLICTS OF INTEREST

Climate change is considered the greatest threat to the tundra and its inhabitants. Global temperatures are increasing faster in the Arctic than in other places on the planet. But different interests have interfered with how effectively the tundra is conserved. A battle has emerged between those concerned with protecting the tundra from thawing and releasing further greenhouse gases and those who wish to profit from the natural resources in the tundra. Scientific facts and reasonable arguments do not seem to play a part in this ongoing dispute, as both sides feel passionately about their points of view and decline to negotiate. The result is that tundra protection depends upon which side has the most influence and power at any moment.

For example, under President Barack Obama's administration from 2008 to 2016, climate change regulations in the United States were a top priority. Stricter air quality standards were enacted. Greenhouse gas emissions from vehicles and industry were reduced. The 2009 Copenhagen Accord and the 2015 Paris Agreement brought successful negotiations to strengthen worldwide reductions in greenhouse gas emissions.

The Donald Trump presidential administration, which came into power in the United States in 2017, abruptly changed direction. In March 2017, President Trump signed an executive order that curbed the government's enforcement of climate regulations. This was done to make it less challenging for companies to adhere to regulations. Trump hoped companies would create more jobs as a result. Trump also declared his intention to withdraw from the Paris Agreement.

The opposite happened in Canada. Canada has vast areas of tundra in its northern reaches. Former Prime Minister Stephen Harper led the Conservative government of Canada from 2006 to 2015. He forbade scientists from talking with the press. His government weakened environmental regulations and reduced funding for research. The cutbacks in funding kept

ARCTIC NATIONAL WILDLIFE REFUGE

In 1960, US President Dwight D. Eisenhower set aside the Arctic National Wildlife Refuge (ANWR) in Alaska. The ANWR is one of the most undisturbed areas on Earth. The refuge is dominated by tundra. Large herds of caribou live there. So do polar bears and musk ox, pictured. Native Alaskan tribes have lived there and depended upon the animals for more than 12,000 years.[5]

The park protects the animals and plants of the area for people now and in the future. In 1980, the US Congress and President Jimmy Carter expanded the refuge to 19.6 million acres (7.9 million ha).[6] The 1980 expansion also designated much of the ANWR as wilderness. The area had to be left in its natural state. This prohibited oil, gas, and mining development. However, Congress could reverse the prohibition in the future, meaning that oil and gas drilling could happen.

When negotiations were complete, 195 countries signed the Paris Agreement.

scientists from tracking huge environmental changes taking place in the Arctic tundra resulting in thawing permafrost.

In late 2015, the Liberal Party of Canada won the Canadian election. Justin Trudeau, the leader of the party, became prime minister. By early 2016, he had started to reverse

Canada's stand on climate change. He established an all-inclusive Canadian framework for combating climate change. Further, he led a delegation to the United Nations climate summit to show Canada was now going to participate in combating climate change. He began new environmental rules on natural resource projects. This included consulting with indigenous peoples on projects affecting them. Trudeau's administration seemed to value preserving and conserving the environment over purely economic gain.

"It's either a vendetta and a total assault on the [sic] anything environmental or a total disinterest in the issue. Whatever it is, I don't think we've seen anything quite like this in Canada."[7]

—Melissa Gorrie, Canadian lawyer for the environmental law group Ecojustice, giving a statement regarding Canadian government environmental actions between 2006 and 2015

One of the biggest roadblocks to preserving the tundra is that countries, businesses, and organizations throughout the world do not cooperate with each other as much as they could. Many countries have attempted to develop international cooperation agreements to combat this challenge. But as of early 2017, there have only been successes on smaller scales.

FOOD WEBS

A large scientific study focused on the Arctic and Antarctic between 2007 and 2009. It was named ArcticWOLVES—Arctic Wildlife Observatories Linking Vulnerable Ecosystems. Its goal was to study how climate change affected tundra food webs. More than 150 scientists and students from nine countries participated in this study.[8] They studied everything from the permafrost under the tundra to the birds flying overhead.

One thing they found was that when the number of large herbivores decreases on the tundra, the food web changes. Canadian national parks have found the number of caribou, which move in and out of the parks, to be decreasing because of climate change. Ground icing after rain or winter thaws reduced the caribous' access to winter eating sites outside the parks. So instead of the usual caribou or musk ox munching on tundra plants, these areas tend to have predators such as foxes and owls munching on smaller animals.

They also found that in some areas small animals, such as the lemming, were the most important plant eaters. They are also the favored prey of Arctic and red foxes, hawks, falcons, owls, weasels, and even grizzly bears. These predators often control the number of lemmings. However, winter weather is playing a growing factor in the supply of these animals. Lots of snow cover usually means lots of lemmings. Less snow or winter melting and freezing due to a warming climate makes it harder for lemmings to burrow into snow for insulation and protection against predators. More lemmings might die, and Arctic foxes would need to find another food source. That might be birds such as Arctic geese. These birds only come to the Arctic in the summer to breed and raise their young. In other words, a warmer climate equals fewer lemmings, which equals hungry predators, and this equals fewer birds.

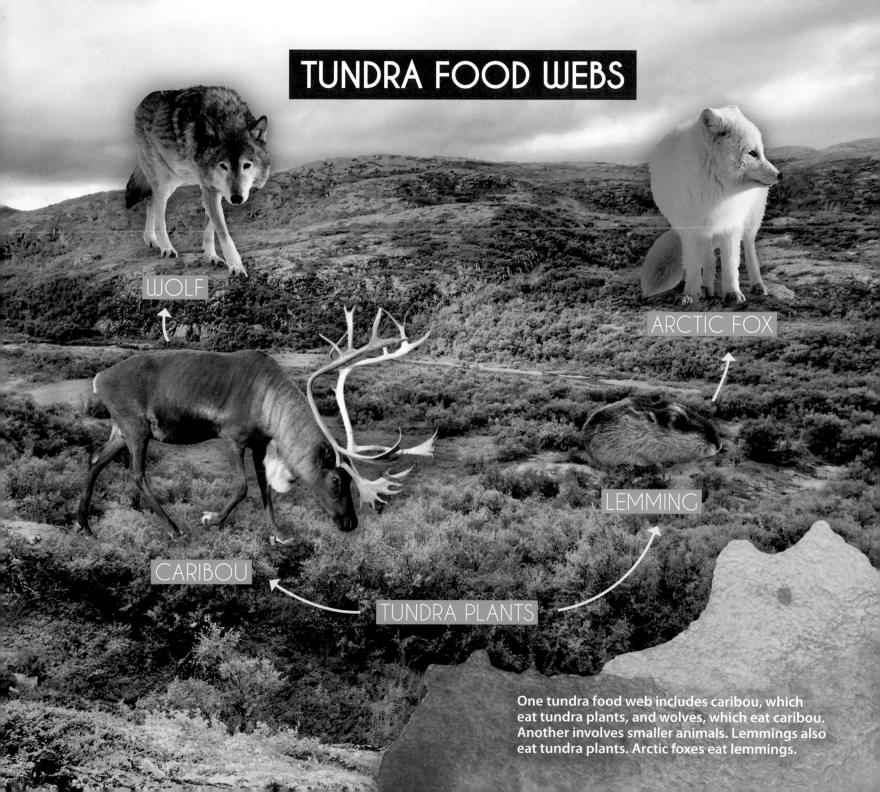

TUNDRA FOOD WEBS

WOLF

ARCTIC FOX

CARIBOU

LEMMING

TUNDRA PLANTS

One tundra food web includes caribou, which eat tundra plants, and wolves, which eat caribou. Another involves smaller animals. Lemmings also eat tundra plants. Arctic foxes eat lemmings.

Protecting tundra areas such as Rocky Mountain National Park can keep ecosystems from being destroyed.

PROACTIVE PREVENTION

While tundra conservation still has a long way to go, many people and organizations are succeeding in conserving portions of it. The best way to ensure the tundra's survival is to stop damage before it starts. The United States has been setting aside protected areas for more than 100 years. Nongovernmental organizations including the World Wildlife Fund, the International Union for Conservation of Nature (IUCN), the Nature Conservancy, and the Sierra Club offer assistance to countries. They have identified potential sites for protection, offered management methods, and provided financial help.

Organizations have been helpful in balancing the struggle between those who want to preserve the tundra's natural beauty and those who want to use its resources. That conflict arose during the 1800s. Some people wanted to restrict human use of protected areas. Others wanted more direct human benefits. It became important to make sure that not just one value or a small group of values prevailed in using the tundra. A way to do this is to identify the major values of a protected area when it is created. These values include water, forest, beauty, or cultural significance. The IUCN created a six-category classification system that is used globally to identify the values of protected areas. This determines how a protected area can be used. Each Arctic country uses a combination of approaches to protect their tundra.

NATURE RESERVES AND WILDERNESS AREAS

The first category identified by the IUCN is strict nature reserves and wilderness areas. Nature reserves protect animal and plant diversity and landscape features. Human usage is strictly controlled to protect the areas. Wilderness areas are typically large, unchanged areas that do not usually have permanent human occupants. They are protected for current and future generations. Also, protected areas preserve past cultural and spiritual values associated with nature. This may include a landmark that holds spiritual significance or an animal a group of people relies on to survive. Scientific studies and educational activities that have a low impact on the areas are strictly managed.

An example of this category is Norway's Svalbard Islands. They are considered one of the last remaining wilderness areas in Europe. The Norwegian government created the Svalbard Environmental Protection Act in 2001 to protect this area. Both the natural environment and cultural heritage of the Russian, Ukrainian, and Polish immigrants to the area, as well as native Norwegians, are at the center of any decisions affecting this area.

NATIONAL PARKS

National parks are the second IUCN category. The parks protect areas with unique landscapes, animals, or plants. National parks are less strict than wilderness areas. They encourage human visits for recreational, spiritual, and educational purposes.

Greenland's National Park is the largest national park in the world. But because it is hard to get to, it is not a national park in the typical sense. No people live in the area except personnel at meteorological stations and a small Danish armed forces unit. Most visitors are part of scientific expeditions or an expedition cruise. Either way, visitors need a government permit. More typical national parks containing either arctic or alpine tundra include Rocky Mountain National Park in Colorado and Sirmilik National Park in Canada.

FINLAND CITIZENS' FAVORITE TUNDRA SPOTS

Celebrating their country's 100 years of independence in 2017, the Finnish Association for Nature Conservation urged Finlanders to name the 100 significant nature sites to preserve for future generations. The project is called 100 Finnish Pearls of Nature. Heikki Susiluoma, the project director, identified one of them as totally on the tundra. Iitto, in northern Lapland, is a landscape that has high peat mounds that contain permafrost. Three other sites that are partially within tundra locations, Lake Inarijärvi, Kätkätunturi, and Suorsapää, were also identified as highly valued by Finland's citizens.

NATURAL MONUMENTS

The third IUCN category is natural monuments or features. These are usually relatively small sites that have a high interest for visitors. However, some sites can be quite large. Caves, rock formations, underwater caverns, and volcanic craters fall in this category. Sacred sites important to certain faith groups and sites important to cultural traditions are also included.

Cape Krusenstern National Monument is located on northwest Alaska's coast with the Chukchi Sea. The site is home to many animals. During the summer season, large numbers of migrating birds come from all over the world to nest. Musk ox can be seen on the tundra surrounding the beach areas. But the cape is most famous for its more than 114 beach ridges along the tundra. Each beach was formed by sediment that the ocean waves left behind. When one beach became high enough that the waves could not wash

Spitsbergen Island is one of the striking locations in Svalbard.

ARCHAEOLOGICAL DISCOVERIES

An archaeology project at the Cape Krusenstern National Monument won a US National Park Service (NPS) award for excellence in 2015. The project took place over six years. It discovered new information about how people from 4,000 years ago interacted with the world around them and with each other. The project demonstrated how 200 generations of people could successfully adapt to the changing environment in northwestern Alaska.

over it anymore, a new beach began forming. While the park protects the ecosystem, it also serves to protect cultural traditions. People would live on the outermost beach, moving up as a new beach formed. They left behind evidence that scientists can use to tell approximately how old a beach is. The ridges formed over the past 9,000 years.[1] Today, the park protects cultural traditions. The Inupiat set up camps in the summer to fish, hunt seal and beluga, and gather other foods. Their people have been doing this for at least 200 generations.

HABITAT AND SPECIES MANAGEMENT AREAS

Habitat or species management areas protect or restore vegetation or animals of local, regional, or international importance. This fourth category includes ocean fishing areas or reindeer habitats. Many of these protected sites would die out without human intervention. People can visit these places and learn about the habitats and what is being done to protect them.

More than 400 kinds of flowers grow on the tundra.[2]

An example of such a management area is in southwestern Alaska. Wolves were found to be seriously threatening caribou populations.

Between 2002 and 2007, one herd of caribou's numbers dropped from 4,200 to 600. No calves were spotted during one calving month in 2007. Wildlife conservation biologists found that the animals were reproducing normally and had sufficient food to survive. However, wolves had made their dens on the calving grounds and were killing the newborn calves. Through three years of culling, the biologists reduced the number of predators by approximately 50 percent, and the caribou populations rebounded to previous numbers.[3] The wolves were not completely removed so the predator to prey ratio became more balanced.

PROTECTED LANDSCAPES AND SEASCAPES

The fifth IUCN category covers protected landscapes and seascapes. This category attempts to balance nature conservation with human activities. These areas are often quite beautiful and have irreplaceable cultural and spiritual value. Recreation and tourism are popular activities in these managed areas.

UMKY PATROL

The World Wildlife Fund and the local villagers of Vankarem, Russia, have created the Umky Patrol. *Umky* means polar bear in the Chukchi language. The people and bears live on an island off the coast of Russia. The collaboration began in order to protect both people and bears. The patrols escort children to school, keep an eye on the bears, and keep locals informed about what's happening. Additionally, the project helps the local people participate in scientific research on bears and other animals.

KEEPING WARM AND COOL

Many animals hibernate through the winter. But tundra animals must adapt to an environment that is cold too long for hibernation. Tundra plants are the food that provides energy for animals living on the tundra. One of the most important animal adaptations is controlling heat loss. Skin radiates heat quickly in very cold temperatures. As the temperature goes down, the loss of body heat goes up. Unprotected skin can quickly lead to hypothermia and death.

Some animals adapt by having a small surface-to-volume ratio. This means they are relatively small with short legs and small ears. Arctic foxes, for example, weigh only 6.5 to 17 pounds (2.9 to 7.7 kg) and have short ears and muzzles.[4]

An insulating layer of fur or feathers can also keep body heat from escaping. Fur or feathers trap air. Air is a poor conductor of heat. This slows the animal's heat loss. During the warmer summer season, winter coats would be too warm. So furry animals such as musk ox often shed some of their fur. Birds do not lose feathers, but they don't fluff their feathers in warmer weather. Fluffing their feathers traps the air that serves as insulation in the winter. Polar bears have thick, insulating fur. It is very oily and repels water, keeping them dryer when they swim. They also have a thick layer of fat under their skin that protects against the cold.

Some animals heat their bodies by increasing their physical activities. Running, digging, and shivering are all ways to do this. To reduce body heat, some animals pant like dogs. The moisture evaporating off their tongues cools them off in the same way sweating cools off people.

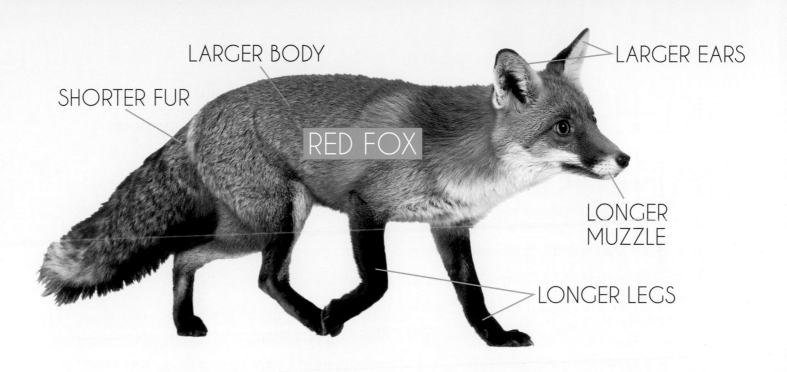

LARGER BODY

LARGER EARS

SHORTER FUR

RED FOX

LONGER MUZZLE

LONGER LEGS

LONGER FUR

SMALLER EARS

SMALLER BODY

ARCTIC FOX

SHORTER MUZZLE

SHORTER LEGS

The Arctic fox's adaptations to the tundra are apparent when compared to a red fox.

One such protected landscape is the Kamchatka Peninsula ecoregion in Russia. The large, diverse ecosystem, including Arctic tundra and alpine tundra, was threatened by uncontrolled visits, fish poaching, and fires. A collaboration between the Global Environment Facility, the United Nations Development Programme, and the Ministry of Natural Resources and Environment of the Russian Federation went to work.

The project's goals were to decrease poaching through policing efforts, develop environmental awareness facilities and programs, and encourage alternative livelihoods for local communities. Results of the project were encouraging. Three visitor centers were built and staffed. They informed tourists and held educational programs for schools, businesses, and the general public. Although poaching within the park areas decreased, it increased outside the boundaries of the park. It was determined that poaching was the result of limited job opportunities. People could not live without the poaching. To address the job issue, environment-friendly, income-creating projects, such as ecotourism businesses and visitor center staffing, now employ local people.

PROTECTED AREAS WITH HUMAN POPULATIONS

The final IUCN category is for managed-resource protected areas. These areas are usually large and involve economic benefits to both companies and the local population. Agreements between local and outside interests preserve much of the existing environment while allowing activities such as mining, drilling, or fishing.

Visitors to Kamchatka Peninsula can see steaming geysers.

The Annapurna Conservation Area in the alpine tundra of Nepal is an example of this category. Begun in 1986, it was the first and largest protected area in Nepal. It has the world's deepest river gorge and a valley with fossils dating from 60 million years ago.[5] The world's largest rhododendron forest is in the area, as is the world's highest altitude fresh water lake. The Annapurna region is culturally diverse. It has at least six unique cultural groups that each speak their own dialect.[6]

All those features make the Annapurna Conservation Area a big tourist destination. But visitors used twice the fuelwood as the local population. This stressed the forest resources. The amount of nonrecyclable waste was growing at a dangerous rate.

A tourism management program began to balance local ecology values, the livelihood needs of the local community, and tourist satisfaction. Alternative energy programs began promoting substitutes for fuelwood as well as more energy-efficient ways to use fuelwood. And activities help local people manage tourism and develop their own tourism businesses.

All these strategies have prevented tundra destruction. They have also encouraged people to work together. Governments and local organizations have come together to preserve these important landscapes.

The Ghandruk village of the Gurung people is in the Annapurna Conservation Area.

Large pieces of trash from the railroad were scattered across the Wild Hart tundra.

Chapter FIVE

CLEANING UP

Sometimes, people have already damaged a tundra ecosystem. Preventing further damage is not enough to keep a healthy ecosystem. Trash and other things will not go away on their own. People need to step in and clean up the area.

In the early 1980s, a train line was constructed. It crossed the Rocky Mountains in northern British Columbia, Canada, in the Wild Hart ranges. The railroad went through two long tunnels to reach coal mines. Because it was close to a hydroelectric dam and transmission lines, the railway became one of a few electrified freight lines in North America. Eventually, the coal mines were abandoned, and the railroad was closed in 2003. But its footprint still affected the environment.

WOLVERINE NORDIC AND MOUNTAIN SOCIETY

The Wolverine Nordic and Mountain Society (WNMS) is a volunteer organization that builds and maintains hiking and cross-country skiing trails near Tumbler Ridge, Canada. One of the goals of the society is to encourage people to get involved in nonmotorized outdoor recreation. The group sponsors several large cross-country running races, which help sustain the Tumbler Ridge economy. WNMS is an example of a group dedicated to promoting respect for the environment while also providing recreational and tourism opportunities for people.

When the two railway tunnels were built, two large towers were also constructed. There was a large collection of batteries in each tower. Those two towers were also abandoned. Years of winter storms and high winds wrecked the towers. Pieces of sheet metal, Styrofoam block, and the batteries were blown across the alpine tundra meadows. Residents were concerned. Over time, the batteries leak toxic chemicals. No one knew how much of these chemicals the tundra had already absorbed.

For ten years, the local community tried to determine who built the towers and who was responsible for the mess left behind. Finally, local citizens, members of the Wolverine Nordic and Mountain Society (WNMS), the Tumbler Ridge UNESCO Global Geopark, and the Yellowstone to Yukon Conservation Initiative banded together to clean up the site. They hired a helicopter and, with community volunteers, collected the batteries and flew them off the alpine tundra for disposal. This made the area safer for the plants and wildlife living there. Caribou had safer grazing land, and fish had cleaner rivers.

THE POLLUTION PROBLEM

In the past, some people saw the tundra as a place without much worth. People dumped waste without worrying about the consequences. Human trash threatens tundra ecosystems. It mars beautiful landscapes, which can cause people to be less interested in visiting them. It also harms local plants and animals.

It would seem that scientists studying animal and plant life on the tundra would be the most respectful visitors to pristine environments. But that was not the case on King George Island in the Antarctic. In 2013, German scientists reported disintegrating work shacks, huge piles of trash, and shorelines slick with oil at the center of the

A helicopter flew trash off the Wild Hart tundra so it could be safely disposed of.

international research site. In some places, this trash had been accumulating since 1968.

Vehicles had driven off defined roadways, and their wheels gouged and destroyed fragile tundra plants. Poisonous chemicals, oilcans, and old car batteries lay exposed in open pits. Scientists brought non-native plants, animals, and insects to the island, probably by accident. Those non-native visitors threatened the very environment the scientists had come to study. On other sites in Antarctica, large sinkable items, such as broken-down vehicles, were taken out onto the sea ice. When summer came and the ice broke up, the vehicles sank into the ocean. Other garbage was taken inland and dropped down deep crevasses.

Even though there were rules regarding trash cleanup for the research sites, they were not followed. Although thousands of tons of waste were removed after the Germans' report came out, the littering

Rusted barrels were left sitting near the shore on King George Island.

TRASH KILLS BEARS

Rocky Mountain National Park in Colorado has alpine tundra within its boundaries. Human food garbage is causing problems for the local bears and the people visiting the park. The bears are very persistent at getting the food. They have even torn the bumpers off cars and broken car windows to get at tasty treats. Once a problem bear becomes accustomed to human food, it will continue to seek it out. It has to be killed or else prevented from reaching the food. One way to prevent bears from reaching food is special garbage cans that have lids with handles that bears cannot open. These are standard features at US protected areas. Common sense about not feeding the bears and putting trash in the proper containers keeps bears from learning to eat human food. Park visitors can store their food in bear-resistant containers away from their campsites. While eating outdoors, they should never turn their back on their food and never leave behind food or food wrappers. Everything that comes into a park must also leave with the visitors.

continued. The authors of the report called for the site to be made an Antarctic Specially Managed Area so that stricter legally binding rules could be enforced. Some doubt this will happen, however, as countries disagree on what the rules should be. At the time of the study, environmental audits were conducted regularly to ensure compliance with environmental laws. Many of the bases have switched to using alternative energy resources, such as wind and solar, to reduce the need for gas and diesel-powered generators. Now, both tundra land and sea ecosystems are better protected.

ALASKA OIL PIPELINE SPILL CLEANUP

Not all tundra cleanup projects happen decades after the damage has been done. Some cleanups start almost immediately. On November 29, 2009, ice formed in a BP pipeline. This blocked the oil and caused a 2-foot (0.6 m) rupture.[1] More than 46,000 gallons (174,000 L) of oil and water sprayed onto the Alaskan tundra below.[2] Because of the freezing temperatures, the spill did not spread too far. But the tundra was at risk. Oil spills can harm the delicate tundra for decades. And the spill also risked traveling to Prudhoe Bay, where it could pollute the water and harm marine life.

BP began evaluating the site and coming up with a cleanup plan that day. The next day, it built a ridge of snow to keep the oil from reaching the bay. BP also began collecting contaminated snow. Cleanup efforts included using steam to loosen the thick mess so it could be vacuumed up. Workers used jackhammers to break off contaminated ice. Heavy equipment also scooped up the oil and frozen water, which were then trucked away. According to a BP spokesperson, the cleanup was "pretty effective."[3] They were able to clean up much of the oil. But the tundra plants below had been destroyed by the oil collection. A more intensive plan would be necessary for the site to return to tundra habitat again.

"If there isn't a profound change of direction, these negative environmental influences will be amplified in the next few years."[4]

—Dr. Hans-Ulrich Peter, an ecologist at the University of Jena and coauthor of the report about waste on Antarctica's King George Island, 2013

LEAKS AND EXPLOSIONS

BP is no stranger to oil leaks and gas explosions in sensitive US areas. In 2006, the largest oil spill ever at Prudhoe Bay, Alaska, occurred at the company's site. It paid more than $20 million in fines and penalties.[5] Six years later, it paid an additional $66 million penalty.[6] On April 20, 2010, the Deepwater Horizon oil rig in the Gulf of Mexico exploded, killing 11 workers. It caused the biggest offshore oil spill in US history. BP predicted the accident would cost it approximately $62 billion by 2019.[7] Then, on July 16, 2011, a spill at their Lisburne field, part of Greater Prudhoe Bay, leaked oily material onto the Alaskan tundra, costing them even more.

The Trans-Alaska Pipeline runs through the Alaska North Slope.

REHABILITATION AND RESTORATION

Cleaning up tundra makes it safer for the plants and animals living there. But some tundra ecosystems have been damaged so badly that more drastic measures are needed. In some areas, human activity has significantly damaged or destroyed a habitat. Without help, the natural tundra might never return. This is the situation in many areas of the Alaska North Slope. Between 2005 and 2015, tundra ecosystems were damaged by gravel pits, roads, airstrips, oil spills, and trenching used to bury cable or pipelines. More than 100 sites needed human intervention.[1]

REHABILITATION

There are two approaches to repairing tundra ecosystems. One is rehabilitation. Rehabilitation is completing enough repairs so that plants and animals can again use the site. These plants and animals are not always the same as the original species before disturbance. The Zimovs' work at the NESS is an example of site rehabilitation.

On the Alaska North Slope, oil companies that were involved in causing tundra disturbances, along with the state of Alaska, collaborated to develop rehabilitation guidelines for gravel roads, pits, and pads. Those guidelines are reviewed by industry partners and federal, state, and local agencies. This approach addresses both economic values and the natural values of the Alaskan tundra.

Oil drill sites clear sections of tundra, which then take a long time to grow back once the operation is finished.

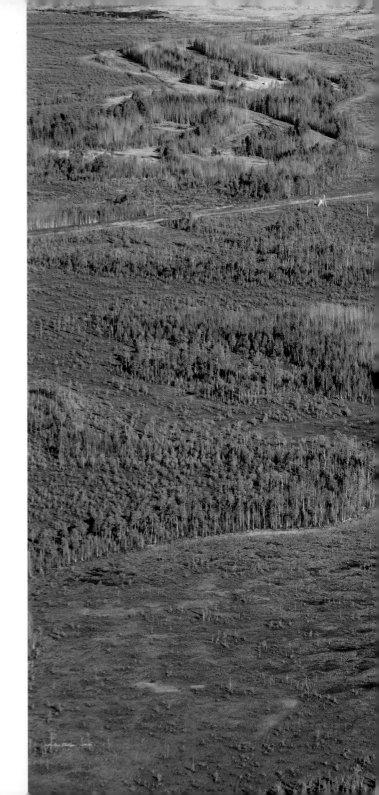

Tires can cause permanent damage to the tundra and expose the ground to warmer summer temperatures, helping thaw permafrost.

One of the guidelines relates to preventing seismic trail damage. To find oil on land, specialized seismic survey trucks that carry a heavy plate are used. The plate is vibrated to create a seismic wave that travels into the ground. That wave bounces off the rocks that contain oil and is measured by instruments on the truck. Once oil is found, drilling rigs are set up to bring the oil to the surface. The heavy survey trucks cause much damage to the fragile tundra on which they drive. A part of the solution is to use low-pressure tires and tracked vehicles that lessen the damage to the tundra. Another solution is to cancel or reduce surveys when there is not enough snow even to protect the tundra from vehicles with low-pressure tires and tracks.

Another guideline deals with rehabilitating the tundra after an oil spill. Oil-saturated soil is dug up and removed.

Gravel is then put into the hole and covered with soil brought in from somewhere else. This approach was found to be very successful at helping plants regrow but also very expensive because the soil had to be put in place by hand. Once an area has been rehabilitated, it may become a full restoration project.

RESTORATION

Restoration is often the second step in recovering an area. It involves bringing back the original animals and plants that were there before the disturbance took place. This attempts to restore the habitat to its original state. Restoration is more difficult than rehabilitation, but it is also the most beneficial in the long run.

THE ALASKA NORTH SLOPE

The Alaska North Slope is a region of northern Alaska. Also known as the Arctic North Slope, it runs north from the base of the Brooks mountain range to the Arctic Ocean. In the late 1960s, large deposits of oil were discovered near Prudhoe Bay. Within ten years, an 800-mile (1,300 km) oil pipeline was built from the north to south coasts of Alaska to carry the oil.[2] A 2003 report on North Slope drilling determined that lasting damage to the tundra had occurred because the harsh climate had slowed natural recovery and also because the oil companies had done little to restore the areas where drilling was completed.

Oil production in Alaska's tundra continues to prompt the need for tundra restoration. Production techniques can cause damage that allows the underlying permafrost to thaw. This thawing causes subsidence, when land collapses in on itself, and greatly hinders new plant growth and the return of native animals. Some have tried to rehabilitate these areas by bringing in non-native plants. But these plants are not suited to the very short tundra growing season. They do not repopulate disturbed areas well. So transplanting tundra sod is a common form of tundra restoration.

The Inupiat of Alaska have long used tundra sodding. Inupiaq elder Charles Hopson used traditional knowledge of tundra sodding to create a method that would effectively restore damaged tundra sites. Transplanted sod consists of mature native plants with complete root systems that can quickly take root in the new location during the short growing season.

There are challenges to the sodding technique. Tundra sod needs to be cut out from an existing tundra ecosystem. People can only gather the sod from sites that are due to be built upon for other purposes. Some places that need sod cannot be accessed with vehicles. People set up a track with rollers to move the heavy pieces. The sod must be placed against other pieces of sod so the soil doesn't dry out quickly. It then needs to be monitored to

A restored habitat has all of the same species of plants and animals that lived there before it was harmed.

ensure it survives. Sodding is expensive and requires a lot of work. But the results make up for the challenges.

In 2010, Hopson and his workers resodded an 11,991-square-foot (1,114 sq m) area that had been damaged from an oil spill cleanup.[3] Previous oil company attempts to revegetate the disturbed area had been unsuccessful. But the sod revegetated the area in a single growing season. The sodding proved that a severely disturbed site could be rehabilitated in a single year, even in the harsh climate of the delicate tundra.

Algae, fungi, and lichens are often lumped in when discussing plants of the tundra. However, scientists do not classify them as plants. They are separate forms of life just as they are named— algae, fungi, and lichen.

Restoration is what the BP oil spill site needed. The company completed a site restoration plan that involved moving tundra sod onto the spill site. The Alaska Department of Environmental Conservation approved the plan. In the summer of 2010, BP would move tundra sod from a construction site and replant it at the spill site, saving those plants from destruction. The sod would bring back healthy tundra plants where the oil spill and its cleanup had destroyed them. The site would be monitored for five years after the spill. BP eventually settled a civil lawsuit that asked BP to pay a fine for oil that had made it into waters around their North Slope pipelines. BP agreed to pay its share of a $450,000 fine.[4] The company did not admit to any wrongdoing.

GOLD MINING CLEANUP IN DENALI NATIONAL PARK AND PRESERVE, ALASKA

Drilling for oil and gas are not the only industrial practices that have caused disturbances in Arctic and alpine tundra. In approximately 1905, gold miners stampeded to what is now part of the Kantishna district of Denali National Park and Preserve in Alaska. The initial gold rush quickly died out, but mining continued until 1985. Some of the miners sifted through the sands of streams to find the gold. Others dug mines, while still others used heavy equipment to gouge out streambeds. Miners often did not clean up after themselves. The National Park Service (NPS) found abandoned camps, mining equipment, ruined floodplains, piles of excess mined materials, and hazardous materials such as arsenic.

In 1989, the NPS began reclamation activities to restore the streambeds and other sites back to some degree of a healthy stream environment. The workers removed hazardous materials, abandoned equipment,

TUNDRA PLANT RESTORATION IS DIFFICULT

Traditional plant restoration on other ecosystems, such as grasslands, has been quite successful using techniques such as seeding. Seeding usually involves fertilizing the area and then scattering grass or tundra plant seed. In seeding, the plants are often left to grow without additional aid. The same is not true for the tundra. Seeding of disturbed Arctic tundra sites has only seen very limited success, even with the use of fertilizers. Tundra plants, such as Arctic poppies, are very slow growing because of the wind and cold temperatures. They are very fragile and slow to recover from damage.

Acidic fluids leaked from an abandoned gold mine in Kantishna.

and contaminated soil. They also rebuilt the damaged floodplains, repaired stream banks to prevent further erosion, and planted vegetation that would help the land recover.

The rehabilitation of the Kantishna Hills has been fairly successful. The water quality in most of the streams has improved. The streams are much clearer, but there are still some traces of arsenic in the streambeds. The revegetated land along the streams has stabilized the ground and prevented more sediment from being washed into the streams. One of the streams, Caribou Creek, was removed from the list of impaired waters in the US Clean Water Act. Impaired waters are streams, rivers, lakes, and ocean areas that do not meet safe water quality guidelines. Once the water quality issues are fixed, a body of water is removed from the list. Work continued on other sites in the Kantishna Hills after 2011.

THE KANTISHNA GOLD RUSH

The Kantishna Gold Rush began approximately eight years after the more famous Klondike Gold Rush of 1896. It happened in what is now Denali National Park and Preserve in Alaska. The Kantishna stampede to the gold area was the result of two gold discoveries that happened at approximately the same time. By 1905, thousands of prospectors had come to the area. Within a few years it became evident that most of the areas with gold were under the control of the two miners who made the first discoveries. Small towns that had sprung up overnight disappeared just as quickly. By 1925, only 13 miners were successfully producing gold.[5] Many prospectors headed home empty handed.

Mining methods changed in the 1930s, and Kantishna again was a successful gold-producing region up until World War II (1939–1945). All gold mining operations were shut down by the government as nonessential wartime industries. After the war, mining continued in Kantishna until the early 1990s. It became part of the Denali National Park and Preserve in 1980, and most of the mining claims now belong to the NPS.

The Svalbard Islands are home to animals including reindeer.

SEVEN

THREATS FROM THE OUTSIDE

The Svalbard Islands off the coast of Norway are pristine wilderness areas. In 1995, a coal company wanted to build a road through the islands' largest tundra area. It would have been the first of many construction projects that would damage the tundra.

A number of nongovernmental organizations and tourism groups started a campaign to stop the road. The campaign was called "No Road through Svalbard Wilderness!" It asked people to send the Norwegian prime minister a postcard to put a halt to the road.

The 4,000 postcards delivered had a tremendous impact on the Norwegian parliament.[1] The parliament placed much of the area under protection as national parks. This saved the tundra and its natural features from harm. Tourism was encouraged. Visitors pay a tourist fee that goes into an environment fund. The fund supports education, cultural heritage activities, nature conservation, and research projects for managing tourism and protected areas. The action by Norway and its people make Svalbard an excellent example of combining natural values with tourism to protect an area.

TUNDRA INVADERS

But humans aren't the only ones harming the tundra. Plants and animals are also attacking the tundra biome. These threats are called invasive species. An invasive species is one that moves into or is brought into an area where it is not native and it outcompetes

Lesser snow geese numbers have been rising in North America. They eat so much tundra vegetation that only fenced-off areas where they don't feed are green.

the original plants and animals. This throws whole ecosystems off-balance. According to the Global Invasive Species Database, there are 15 invasive species in the tundra.[2] Dogs, cats, weasels, and red foxes all prey on small animals such as lemmings, which are the basic food of tundra predators. The local animals, such as Arctic foxes and snowy owls, have a much more difficult time surviving when their main food source is harder to find.

Canada geese have become an invasive species in some areas. These once short-term summer visitors now stay longer on the tundra and overgraze the plants and insects living there. This takes food away from the other birds and animals that depend upon the sites for food. Starlings are another species that compete with native birds for food and shelter. They reproduce so quickly that their numbers increase more rapidly than the native species' populations.

Canada geese can be found in the tundra in Northern Quebec, Canada.

TREE INVASION

Climate change is predicted to increase the growth of trees and shrubs in Scandinavia by 2070. This increase is at the expense of the tundra biome. Without trees, the tundra's winter snows reflect much of the heat away from the ground. But trees and shrubs absorb warmth, allowing the tundra to get warmer than usual. The warming encourages more tree growth, and the cycle continues.

Plant-eating animals, including reindeer, can help prevent tree growth. When reindeer graze on newly growing trees and taller shrubs at the edges of the tundra in June and July, they help keep the tundra open. Halting the tree invasion would help decrease the warming trend of climate change and protect the tundra.

A separate study by the Arctic Council found that more than 12 invasive plant species have moved onto the tundra in Canada.[3] Invasive species threaten the delicate balance of tundra ecosystems. But various governments and organizations have started successful programs to remove or control the invaders.

INVASIVE CATS

Marion Island, off the coast of South Africa, is in the Southern Indian Ocean islands tundra biome. The island is a territory of South Africa. Because it is so isolated, there are few species of birds, animals, and plants. This lack of diversity leaves native species very vulnerable to aggressive imported species.

In 1949, the house cat was introduced to Marion Island. People originally brought cats in to control the mice population at a weather station. Little did these people know that the cats preferred the island's birds to mice. The cats only ate the mice when the birds were not around. The cats caused one bird species to disappear entirely from the island. Three other bird species were near disappearing when South African authorities stepped in.

The authorities were able to successfully remove all the cats from the island. They trapped, poisoned, and shot cats. They also released a viral disease to kill the cats. By 1991, no cats were seen. This was the first time cats had been eliminated from a subantarctic island. The bird species that had disappeared returned to the island. The other bird species have recovered as well. Now, the other invasive species, the mouse, has become the target of removal. It damages plants and eats insects that nourish the birds and other plants. The mouse population appears to be increasing because of climate change and the removal of the cats.

Pine trees are an invasive species in the Siberian Arctic biome. The trees were originally planted to increase forest size and habitats for some animals. But they use up the nutrients and block sunlight that the native tundra plants need to survive.

CROSS-COUNTRY COLLABORATION

The tundra areas of Europe are located and connected in the Scandinavian countries Sweden, Finland, and Norway. These countries are comparatively small and closely bunched. Successful tundra conservation projects naturally involve collaboration between two or more of the countries.

The Arctic fox is one example of collaborative conservation. The fox lives in the frozen northern tundra areas of Scandinavia. The fox can survive in that climate because of its metabolism, insulating fur, and small size and shape. These all help reduce energy loss. It can also go a long time without eating.

As the red fox invaded the tundra, Arctic foxes needed help to reproduce and thrive.

In the early 1800s, more than 10,000 Arctic foxes lived in Scandinavia. In the 1800s and 1900s, the Arctic fox was hunted extensively for its beautiful white fur. The number of foxes declined dramatically. Sweden eventually protected the animal in 1928. Norway followed in 1930 and then Finland in 1940. But still, the Arctic fox population did not recover or even increase. In 2011, there were only approximately 80 adult foxes in Norway, 120 in Sweden, and 6 occasionally sighted in Finland.[4] The fox was identified as a critically endangered species. This meant it was in danger of disappearing completely from the Scandinavian tundra.

One of the reasons for the lagging Arctic fox recovery is that the larger red fox is moving into its tundra territory. The red fox's larger size and lower cold tolerance used to keep it out of Arctic fox territory. But with the warming climate, the red fox can now survive in its smaller relative's home. The Arctic fox was pushed into territory where survival was more difficult.

Norway and Sweden started a three-pronged approach to restoring the Arctic fox to its tundra range. First, they began reestablishing extinct or small populations. They bred pups in captivity and then released them in the natural fox environment. Between 2006 and 2011, approximately 217 pups were released into the wild.[5] The pups exceeded all expectations when more than one-half survived their first year.

The second and third steps had to be done together. Early on, the Arctic foxes needed supplementary feeding to survive and reproduce. But putting out food for the Arctic

Released Arctic foxes need feeders as they get used to hunting for their food in case they cannot catch enough to survive.

foxes also attracted the red foxes. So red foxes were removed from the areas where the supplementary feeding was taking place. The collaboration between Norway and Sweden has helped reestablish the Arctic fox. However, Scandinavia's 2011 population was slightly more than 200. That needs to increase to more than 500 to call it a long-lasting success.[6]

"It is important to predict which native species are most at risk and to monitor their populations so that if they start to decline catastrophically, we can establish captive breeding programs and other supportive measures."[7]

—*Vladimir Dinets, a researcher studying the effects of climate change on wildlife, quoted after seeing dramatic changes in the Bering Strait landscape, 2015*

CONTROLLING INVASIVE SPECIES

There is a three-step approach to controlling any invasive species, not just those on the tundra. The first step is to prevent the importation of species. The second step is to eradicate any species that has already arrived. The third step, if all else fails, is to contain the spread of the species and limit its numbers. These three steps have been applied in Norway and many other countries that try to combat invasive species.

An Oyer, Norway, dam creates hydroelectric energy.

OUTLOOK FOR THE TUNDRA

Preserving the tundra and its permafrost could prevent a drastic increase in climate change. So countries throughout the world have acted to help reduce greenhouse gas emissions. Iceland, Norway, Finland, and Sweden have all begun reducing the greenhouse gas emissions they produce. They replace fossil fuels with alternative energy, such as hydroelectric energy. Sweden taxed oil-based heating and offered incentives to encourage energy producers to switch to renewable electric energy production.

ALL-ELECTRIC POWERED SHIP

One way to combat climate change is to switch from using fossil fuels to electricity to power cars, trucks, and ships. Yara, a Norwegian company, is planning to use electricity to power its local container ships. Not only will the ship be all electric, it will also eventually be self driving.

Yara currently transports its products across Norway by truck. Eliminating the 40,000 truck trips a year will greatly reduce the carbon dioxide produced by the company.[2] Moving from the roads to the sea will also make roads safer and reduce noise and pollution.

RESTORE, PRESERVE, OR ADAPT

Even though some countries are reducing their emissions, at some point, returning the tundra to its original condition may not be possible. And some question when to stop with conservation. Catherine West, a research assistant professor from Boston University, questioned what the goal of conservation and restoration of the landscape is. She had just completed researching whether a ground squirrel on an Alaskan island was invasive. The island also has non-native cattle and Arctic foxes. She asked, "If we eradicate the cattle, we get back to a landscape that was precattle, but it had foxes on it. So then do we eradicate the foxes to get back to the prefox landscape? Okay, then we get back to a landscape where native people were using this island heavily? Do we go back, then, to before native people came to the island?"[1]

Removing people from tundra habitats is not an option. What West was saying is that, at some point, going back to the way things were can't be done.

Some animals that originally lived in the tundra, such as the wooly mammoth, are extinct. We cannot reintroduce them to the tundra. The task then becomes reducing additional damage as much as possible and adapting to the way things are.

Marlow Pellatt, an ecosystem scientist for Parks Canada, agrees. In a 2014 presentation, he suggested that reducing the sources of climate change was very important. But he also indicated that growing levels of carbon dioxide already released into the air since the 1800s means adaptation to climate change needs to be at the top of conservation actions.

CHANGES IN ALASKA BY 2100

If things continue the way they are currently going, scientific computer models predict that northern Alaska will be wetter and warmer by the year 2100. This means more grasses, shrubs, and taller trees. Water-based systems, including streams and lakes, could be more productive but may dry as warmer temperatures lead to more evaporation. The models also suggest the large changes on land could be associated with permafrost thaw and lead to drastic changes in the tundra ecosystem.

IS ADAPTING GIVING UP?

Dr. John All is an environmental scientist and mountain climber. During an interview in 2017, he was asked about adapting to climate change. He said if people really wanted to stop climate change completely, the world would have to stop the use of all fossil fuels immediately. Dr. All did not think that would happen in the near future. Instead, he thought two things could be done. The first was to find ways to use less fossil

A US government report found that 86 percent of Alaskan native villages were at risk from the changing climate.[3]

fuels. The second was to realize the world is changing and that adaptations can be made.

Dr. All went on to say that people should not just look at how the climate is changing. He said it was important to look at how societies already adapt to present climate conditions and use those methods in the future. For instance, looking at people in Central America who deal with frequent hurricanes can be helpful for those farther north who may experience more frequent hurricanes in the future.

BLUEPRINT FOR ADAPTING

Adapting to a changing climate should not be a spur-of-the-moment undertaking. A thoughtful and scientifically sound process should be followed. Such guidance for protected areas throughout the world already exists. The IUCN partnered with environmental organizations and protected areas throughout the world to develop guidelines for

Some tourists help pick up trash when they visit tundra areas.

"The clear and present danger of climate change means we cannot burn our way to prosperity. We already rely too heavily on fossil fuels. We need to find a new, sustainable path to the future we want. We need a clean industrial revolution."[4]

—Ban Ki-moon, United Nations secretary general, 2011

adapting to a changing climate. The guidelines were published in 2016 and are considered examples of the best ways to help protected areas cope with change.

The guidelines presented five steps to increase the success of adapting. The first step is to gather the best information possible and identify the tools to help the adaptations. This step also involves planning for change. The second step is measuring what species, ecosystems, and other values are most at risk. Thirdly, the organization must choose the actions they will take to assist in saving the protected area and adapting to change. The fourth step is to act on those plans. The last step is to measure whether the actions are a success or failure. Then, the protected

If countries work together, tundra ecosystems will be healthy for generations to come.

area managers can decide what further actions might be needed. These guidelines serve as a road map for adapting to a changing environment.

CAUSES FOR OPTIMISM AMID UNCERTAINTY

There is reason for optimism about protecting the Arctic even with growing pressures on that landscape. Protected areas and legislation are changing to include the economic and natural values of local people, indigenous cultures, and the business sector. And people are working together to help save threatened tundra areas.

Several regional groups have formed to protect the Arctic. The Nordic Council of Ministers developed an Arctic action plan that reviewed protected areas in the five Nordic countries. The Arctic is one of the protected areas included in the European Union's Natura 2000 initiative. Natura 2000 is the world's largest coordinated network of protected areas. It provides protection for all of the most valued and threatened species and habitats in the 28 European Union countries.[5] The Barents Euro-Arctic Cooperation organization seeks to link protected areas in northwest Russia and the Barents portion of Scandinavia. Between 1992 and 2017, many countries have also come together and said they would work to end climate change. They have come up with targets to reduce emission levels. But despite all the meetings and agreements, climate change with its effects on the tundra continues.

Taking care of the tundra will help plants and animals, including the Arctic ground squirrel, thrive.

SUCCESSFULLY PROTECTING THE TUNDRA

Across the planet, actions to protect the tundra environment continue to be successful. Balancing people's needs and natural values can be and has been accomplished. The trick is recognizing problems and determining effective ways to solve them.

The other necessary ingredient is cooperation. A willingness to hear another side of the story is necessary. Will countries, local communities, and individuals do what is fair for the entire planet and the tundra? Or will they focus on only national or personal concerns? That question has yet to be answered in full.

CAUSE AND EFFECT

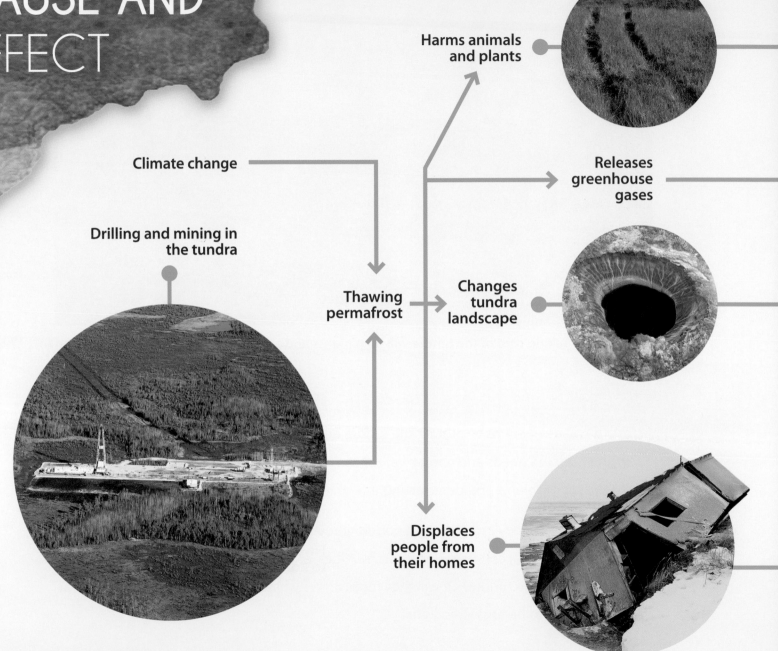

Climate change

Drilling and mining in the tundra

Thawing permafrost

Harms animals and plants

Releases greenhouse gases

Changes tundra landscape

Displaces people from their homes

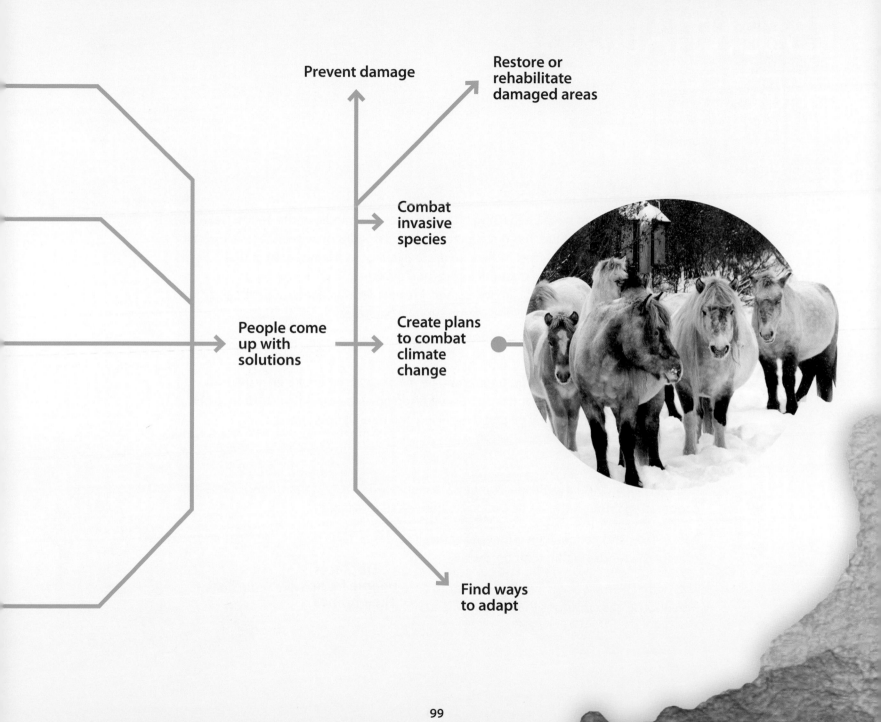

Prevent damage

Restore or
rehabilitate
damaged areas

Combat
invasive
species

People come
up with
solutions

Create plans
to combat
climate
change

Find ways
to adapt

ESSENTIAL
FACTS

WHAT IS HAPPENING

The world's temperatures have been rising bit by bit since the middle of the 1800s. However, the tundra biome's temperature has been increasing approximately twice as fast as the rest of the world. As a result, permafrost is thawing in some areas. As the permafrost thaws, it has the potential to release immense quantities of carbon dioxide and methane gases into the atmosphere. This would speed up climate change. Meanwhile, the plants, animals, and humans who call the tundra home are under increasing survival pressures.

THE CAUSES

There are two main causes of tundra problems. The major cause is climate change from greenhouse gas emissions. A second—but less widespread—cause is the disturbance of the fragile top layers of the tundra by oil and gas drilling and mining operations.

KEY PLAYERS

- Canada, Finland, Iceland, Russia, Norway, Denmark, Sweden, and the United States are cooperating through the Arctic Council to address tundra issues.

- Local, state, and national governments of these countries have developed rules and acted to protect the tundra within their borders.

- The United Nations holds yearly meetings to encourage the worldwide reduction of greenhouse gas emissions that greatly threaten the tundra.

WHAT IS BEING DONE TO FIX THE DAMAGE

Individual countries set aside areas such as national parks and wilderness areas to prevent damage to the tundra. Where damage has already occurred, restoration, rehabilitation, and invasive species projects attempt to remedy the situation. Local, national, and international actions continue to be undertaken to control climate change.

WHAT IT MEANS FOR THE FUTURE

If climate change continues, scientists expect eroding coastlines and extreme weather patterns. International cooperation and immediate action can reduce future problems. Some people believe we must start planning now to adapt to significant environmental changes in the near future.

QUOTE

"The Arctic region, the barometer of global climate change, is like an environmental early warning system of the world."

—*Klaus Töpfer, executive director of the United Nations Environment Programme, 2004*

GLOSSARY

ADAPT

To adjust to different conditions.

COLLABORATE

To work on a project jointly.

CONSERVATION

The preservation, protection, or restoration of the natural environment.

CULL

To control a population's numbers by killing some.

DIALECT

A form of a language that is spoken in one area of a country or by a social group.

EMISSIONS

The production and discharge of something, especially gas or radiation.

EXTINCT

Having no living members.

FOOD WEB

A system of interlocking food chains.

HABITAT

The natural environment of an organism.

HERBIVORE

A plant-eating animal.

HYPOTHERMIA

The condition of having an abnormally low body temperature.

INDIGENOUS

Originating in or native to a place.

OPTIMISM

Hopefulness and confidence about the future.

PERMAFROST

Permanently frozen soil characteristic of the tundra biome.

PROACTIVE

To take action before something happens rather than waiting to respond after something happens.

REWILDING

Restoring an area to its original state.

SEISMIC

Relating to vibration through the ground.

ULTRAVIOLET

A type of electromagnetic radiation.

ADDITIONAL RESOURCES

SELECTED BIBLIOGRAPHY

"Arctic Fox." *National Geographic*. National Geographic, 2017. Web. 4 Aug. 2017.

Hamilton, Jill, ed. *The Practical Naturalist: Explore the Wonders of the Natural World*. New York: DK, 2010. Print.

Hjorthol, Lars Martin. "Climate: A Challenging Type of Justice." *ScienceNordic*. ScienceNordic, 28 Nov. 2015. Web. 4 Aug. 2017.

Pagnan, Jeanne, et al. "Protected Areas of the Arctic: Conserving a Full Range of Values." *CAFF*. CAFF, 2002. Web. 4 Aug. 2017.

FURTHER READINGS

Henningfeld, Diane Andrews. *Nature and Wildlife*. Detroit, MI: Greenhaven, 2011. Print.

Mara, Wil. *Inside the Oil Industry*. Minneapolis, MN: Abdo, 2017. Print.

Sloan, Christopher. *Baby Mammoth Mummy: Frozen in Time! A Prehistoric Animal's Journey into the 21st Century*. Washington, DC: National Geographic, 2011. Print.

ONLINE RESOURCES

To learn more about tundra conservation, visit **abdobooklinks.com**. These links are routinely monitored and updated to provide the most current information available.

MORE INFORMATION

For more information on this subject, contact or visit the following organizations:

Denali National Park and Preserve

PO Box 9
Denali Park, AK 99755
907-683-9532
nps.gov/dena/index.htm

Denali National Park and Preserve protects a region of Alaskan alpine tundra and the animals in it.

The National Geographic Museum and Headquarters

1145 17th Street NW
Washington, DC 20036
202-857-7700
nationalgeographic.org/dc/plan

The National Geographic Society helps people see the world through the eyes of an explorer. It has information on how technology is being used to protect and explore planet Earth.

SOURCE NOTES

CHAPTER 1. TUNDRA: THE COLDEST ENVIRONMENT

1. Eli Kintisch. "Born to Rewild: A Father and Son Seek to Transform the Arctic and Save the World." *Pulitzer Center*. Pulitzer Center, 9 Dec. 2015. Web. 15 Sept. 2017.

2. Ibid.

3. "Tundra." *National Geographic*. National Geographic Partners, 2017. Web. 15 Sept. 2017.

4. Eli Kintisch. "Born to Rewild: A Father and Son Seek to Transform the Arctic and Save the World." *Pulitzer Center*. Pulitzer Center, 9 Dec. 2015. Web. 15 Sept. 2017.

5. Ibid.

6. "Tundra Biome." *BioExpedition*. BioExpedition, 3 Apr. 2012. Web. 15 Sept. 2017.

7. Peter D. Moore. *Tundra*. New York: Facts on File, 2008. *Google Book Search*. Web. 15 Sept. 2017.

8. Ilekea S. "Tundra Climate." *Blue Planet Biomes*. Blue Planet Biomes, 2000. Web. 15 Sept. 2017.

9. John E. Hobbie and George W. Kling, eds. *Alaska's Changing Arctic: Ecological Consequences for Tundra, Streams, and Lakes*. New York: Oxford UP, 2014. Print. 304.

10. "Global Climate Change: Evidence and Causes." *Down to Earth Climate Change*. University of California-Riverside, n.d. Web. 15 Sept. 2017.

CHAPTER 2. WHAT'S HAPPENING?

1. J. Richter-Menge, J. E. Overland, and J. Mathis. "Arctic Report Card: Update for 2016, Executive Summary." *Arctic Program*. NOAA, 6 Dec. 2016. Web. 15 Sept. 2017.

2. "Tundra." *National Geographic*. National Geographic Partners, 2017. Web. 15 Sept. 2017.

3. J. Richter-Menge, J. E. Overland, and J. Mathis. "Arctic Report Card: Update for 2016, Executive Summary." *Arctic Program*. NOAA, 6 Dec. 2016. Web. 15 Sept. 2017.

4. "World Must Act Now to Forestall Staggering Threat from Global Warming—UN." *UN News Centre*. United Nations, 8 Nov. 2004. Web. 15 Sept. 2017.

5. Wynne Parry. "Global Warming: Arctic Tundra's Climate Change Turns Shrubs Into Trees." *Huffington Post*. Huffington Post, 4 June 2012. Web. 15 Sept. 2017.

6. Patricia Cochran, et al. "Alaska." *National Climate Assessment*. Global Change, 2014. Web. 15 Sept. 2017.

7. Terrence McCoy. "Two New Mysterious Craters Emerge in Siberia Deepening Giant Hole Saga." *Washington Post*. Washington Post, 29 July 2014. Web. 15 Sept. 2017.

8. Steve Visser and John Newsome. "Alaskan Village Votes to Relocate Over Global Warming." *CNN*. Cable News Network, 18 Aug. 2016. Web. 15 Sept. 2017.

9. John Platt. "What Is Methane and Why Should You Care?" *Mother Nature Network*. Narrative Content Group, 11 May 2017. Web. 15 Sept. 2017.

10. "Arctic Report Card." *Arctic Program*. NOAA, 2017. Web. 15 Sept. 2017.

11. Trevor Hughes. "Alaska's Permafrost Threatened by Intense Fires, Climate Change." *USA Today*. USA Today, 14 Aug. 2015. Web. 15 Sept. 2017.

12. Chris Mooney. "Thanks to Global Warming, Antarctica Is Beginning to Turn Green." *Washington Post*. Washington Post, 18 May 2017. Web. 15 Sept. 2017.

13. Matthew Cousens. "EES Week 9: White Gold—The Hope for Those at the Forefront of Climate Change." *Unrepresented Nations and Peoples Organization*. UNPO, 8 Apr. 2009. Web. 15 Sept. 2017.

CHAPTER 3. TUNDRA VALUES

1. Page Spencer, et al. "Protected Areas of the Arctic: Conserving a Full Range of Values." Ottawa, Canada: Conservation of Arctic Flora and Fauna, 2002. 1. *Arctic Portal*. Web. 15 Sept. 2017.

2. Ibid.

3. Jessica Fries-Galther. "Plants of the Arctic and Antarctic." *Beyond Penguins and Polar Bears*. Ohio State University, Mar. 2009. Web. 15 Sept. 2017.

4. "Protected Areas in the Arctic Region." *Arctic Council*. Arctic Council, 12 Jan. 2017. Web. 18 Sept. 2017.

5. "Arctic National Wildlife Refuge." *Full Option Science System*. Regents of the University of California, 2017. Web. 18 Sept. 2017.

6. "Protecting the Arctic National Wildlife Refuge." *National Wildlife Refuge Association*. National Wildlife Refuge Association, 2017. Web. 18 Sept. 2017.

7. Ed Struzik. "Oh Canada: The Government's Broad Assault on Environment." *Yale Environment 360*. Yale University, 2 July 2012. Web. 18 Sept. 2017.

8. G. Gauthier and D. Berteaux, eds. "ArcticWOLVES: Arctic Wildlife Observatories Linking Vulnerable EcoSystems—Final Synthesis Report." Quebec City, Quebec: Centre d'Etudes Nordiques, Universite Laval, 2011. 111. *Centre d'Etudes Nordiques*. Web. 18 Sept. 2017.

CHAPTER 4. PROACTIVE PREVENTION

1. "The Beach Ridges of the Cape." *National Park Service*. US Department of the Interior, 2 Sept. 2017. Web. 18 Sept. 2017.

2. "What Is Tundra Biome?" *Conserve Energy Future*. Conserve Energy Future, 2017. Web. 18 Sept. 2017.

3. "Stories of Success." *Division of Wildlife Conservation*. Alaska Department of Fish & Game, Jan. 2014. Web. 18 Sept. 2017

4. "Arctic Fox." *National Geographic*. National Geographic Partners, 2017. Web. 18 Sept. 2017.

5. "Annapurna Conservation Area Project." *National Trust for Nature Conservation*. National Trust for Nature Conservation, n.d. Web. 18. Sept. 2017.

6. Ibid.

SOURCE
NOTES *CONTINUED*

CHAPTER 5. CLEANING UP

1. Associated Press. "Oil Spill on Alaska Tundra Tied to Frozen Pipe." *NBC News*. NBC News, 10 Dec. 2009. Web. 18 Sept. 2017.

2. "Alaska Spills Highlight Ever-Present Risks from Oil Industry." *PEW Charitable Trusts*. PEW Charitable Trusts. 10 May 2010. Web. 18 Sept. 2017.

3. Associated Press. "Oil Spill on Alaska Tundra Tied to Frozen Pipe." *NBC News*. NBC News, 10 Dec. 2009. Web. 18 Sept. 2017.

4. Mohi Kumar. "Trash Threatens Fragile Antarctic Environment." *Smithsonian Magazine*. Smithsonian, 12 Feb. 2013. Web. 18 Sept. 2017.

5. Nathan Bomey. "BP's Deepwater Horizon Costs Total $62B." *USA Today*. USA Today, 14 July 2016. Web. 18 Sept. 2017.

6. "Alaska to Collect $255m for BP Pipeline Leaks." *Telegraph*. Telegraph Media Group, 9 Nov. 2012. Web. 18 Sept. 2017.

7. "A History of BP's US Disasters." *Telegraph*. Telegraph Media Group, 15 Nov. 2012. Web. 18 Sept. 2017.

CHAPTER 6. REHABILITATION AND RESTORATION

1. "Issues: Rehabilitation and Restoration of Disturbed Tundra." *North Slope Science Initiative*. NSSI, 2015. Web. 18 Sept. 2017.

2. "Alaska North Slope." *Encyclopedia*. Encyclopedia.com, 2016. Web. 18 Sept. 2017.

3. Timothy C. Cater, Charles Hopson, and Bill Streever. "The Use of the Inupiaq Technique of Tundra Sodding to Rehabilitate Wetlands in Northern Alaska." *Arctic Institute of North America*. University of Calgary, 2015. Web. 18 Sept. 2017.

4. Tom Zankl. "Feds, Alaska Agree to $450K Settlement Over BP Oil Spills." *Law360*. Portfolio Media, 25 July 2014. Web. 18 Sept. 2017.

5. Ann Kain and Phil Brease. "Going for the Gold in Kantishna." *National Park Service*. US Department of the Interior, 11 Aug. 2017. Web. 18 Sept. 2017.

CHAPTER 7. THREATS FROM THE OUTSIDE

1. Peter Krokosch. "Svalbard." *Linking Tourism and Conservation*. LT&C, 5 Mar. 2015. Web. 18 Sept. 2017.

2. "What Are Invasive Species in the Tundra?" *Reference*. IAC Publishing, 2017. Web. 18 Sept. 2017.

3. Hans Meltofte, et al. "Arctic Biodiversity Assessment 2013: Synthesis." *Conservation of Arctic Flora and Fauna*. Arctic Council, 2013. Web. 18 Sept. 2017.

4. "The Arctic Fox: A Threatened Species in the Scandinavian Mountains." *Felles Fjellrev*, 2012. 17. *Lansstyrelsen Jamtlands lan*. Web. 18 Sept. 2017.

5. Ibid. 25.

6. Ibid. 28.

7. Samantha Mathewson. "Invasive Species and Climate Change: Eurasian Cuckoos Cross the Bering Strait." *Nature World News*. Nature World News, 17 Sept. 2015. Web. 18 Sept. 2017.

CHAPTER 8. OUTLOOK FOR THE TUNDRA

1. Ian Evans. "Arctic Squirrels: Invasive or Native Species?" *Boston University Research*. Boston University, 17 Feb. 2017. Web. 17 Sept. 2017.

2. Rich Haridy. "World's First All-Electric Autonomous Container Ship to Set Sail in 2018." *New Atlas*. Gizmag, 10 May 2017. Web. 18 Sept. 2017.

3. Suzanne Goldenberg. "America's First Climate Refugees." *Guardian*. Guardian, 2013. Web. 18 Sept. 2017.

4. UN Secretary-General Ban Ki-moon. "Secretary-General Urges Governments to Take Long-Term View on Renewable Energy, Spelling Out Priorities at 'Clean Industrial Revolution' Event in Durban." *United Nations*. United Nations, 6 Dec. 2011. Web. 18 Sept. 2017.

5. "Natura 2000." *European Commission*. European Commission, 27 Apr. 2017. Web. 18 Sept. 2017.

INDEX

ABOUT THE
AUTHOR

Michael Regan, MEd, worked for 30 years as a middle school and college counselor and adviser before turning his attention to research and writing. He is especially interested in topics related to technology and current events. He lives in the southwestern United States.

ABOUT THE CONSULTANT

Professor Jeffrey Welker is the UArctic Research Chair. He has been studying Arctic ecosystems in Alaska, Canada, Greenland, Svalbard, Sweden, and now in Finland most of his professional career. He specializes in the Arctic water cycle, Arctic food webs, greenhouse gas processes, and studies of the Arctic Ocean from the US Coast Guard's icebreaker *Healy*. Dr. Welker uses specialized tools to unravel the mysteries of the Arctic. For example, he uses stable isotope geochemistry and GPS collars on polar bears, wolves, caribou, brown bears, and migratory birds to learn where they go and what they eat.